The open mouth invites the foot. On radio and TV, in pulpit, parliament and classroom, in everyday conversation, people are prone to attacks of FOOT IN MOUTH. The affliction takes many forms – schoolboy howlers, announcers' boobs, social clangers, newspaper misprints. Nigel Rees, who features such slips as part of his popular radio programme 'Quote ... Unquote', has a notable nose for the quotable quote. Here, to follow his best-selling volumes of graffiti and eavesdroppings, he gathers a garland not merely of verbal gaffes but of sayings which are unintentionally hilarious and occasionally inspired.

Also by Nigel Rees in Unwin Paperbacks

'Quote . . . Unquote'
'Quote . . . Unquote 2'
Graffiti Lives, OK
Graffiti 2
Graffiti 3
Graffiti 4
Very Interesting . . . But Stupid!
Eavesdroppings

Published in hardback by
George Allen & Unwin
Slogans

FOOT IN MOUTH

by Nigel Rees

London
UNWIN PAPERBACKS
Boston   Sydney

First published in Unwin Paperbacks 1982

UNWIN® PAPERBACKS
40 Museum Street, London, WC1A 1LU, UK

Unwin Paperbacks,
Park Lane, Hemel Hempstead, Herts HP2 4TE, UK

George Allen & Unwin Australia Pty Ltd.,
8 Napier Street, North Sydney, NSW 2060, Australia

This edition ©Nigel Rees Productions Ltd. 1982

ISBN 0 04 827073 3

Designed by The Small Back Room

Cover illustration by Korky Paul

Typeset by APT Photoset in
VIP Garamond book condensed 11pt and
Futura book 10pt

Printed by
Richard Clay (Chaucer Press) Ltd., Bungay

PREFACE

FOOT IN MOUTH is the umbrella title given to a whole range of verbal gaffes we delight in drawing attention to on the radio programme *Quote ... Unquote*. A 'foot in mouth' is not just a social clanger dropped in conversation. It can arise in one of those classic categories: Malapropisms, Spoonerisms, Goldwynisms or (more recently) Gielgudisms. Or it can occur as a notice or sign, in a note to teacher, over the air as a broadcasting 'boob', or as a misprint in a newspaper. A 'foot in mouth' is not just an error, however. Ideally, it is an inspired error.

I'll try and give you an example of what I mean. After we have recorded an edition of *Quote ... Unquote* – and we always record about ten minutes more material than we need so that the whole programme can be tightened up – the tape is transcribed. This makes the producer's job much easier during editing. The transcribers do not have a very enviable task as they try and render in sensible prose the ravings of sundry show-offs, all speaking at once. But their partial hearings can give rise to some very intriguing scripts. On one occasion when we had Terry Wogan as a guest he used the idiom, 'Groves of Academe'. To my delight, this emerged on the printed page as 'Groves of *Aberdeen*.'

On another show, when John Mortimer was telling an involved anecdote about Alfred Lunt and Lynn Fontanne, the famous theatrical couple came out as 'Alfred Lunt in Linford, Hants.'

MALAPROPISMS are, of course, named after the wonderful character 'Mrs Malaprop' in Sheridan's play *The Rivals* (1775) who has an unerring instinct for choosing the wrong word – 'headstrong as an allegory on the banks of the Nile', 'the very pineapple of politeness', and so on. Shakespeare and Smollet had seized upon this quite common human failing before him but it was Sheridan who named the complaint, employing the French phrase *mal à propos*, meaning 'inopportunely, inappropriately.' From the contents of this book you will be left in no doubt that Mrs Malaprop is alive and well wherever English is spoke. A bookseller in Leicester was asked, 'Have you got Thomas Hardy's *Tess of the Dormobiles?*' Further examples appear as **SCHOOLBOY HOWLERS**.

When we come to **SPOONERISMS**, named after the Revd William Spooner (1844-1930), Warden of New College, Oxford, who was given to transposing the beginnings of words, it is good to find so many of his fellow clergymen still maintaining the tradition – and being big enough to admit it. I am not qualified to say why it is that some people are particularly prone to this form of word-blindness. There is the story of the man who had drunk too much drink at lunch and was stopped by the police as he drove to his office. 'The main thing,' he thought hazily, 'is to be polite.' As the police officer bent down to look in the car, the driver flexed his face muscles and said, 'Good consternoon, affable'. But spoonerising can just as likely occur when you are not under the affluence of incohol.

Many of the Revd Spooner's most famous utterances are probably apocryphal though James Laver, the late fashion historian, once assured me he had heard from Spooner's own lips the phrase, 'Through a dark glassly...' One is tempted to ask: if Dr Spooner had been an ornithologist, would he have called himself a word-botcher? The point is, of course, that he did not just botch words, he did so delightfully. As did Ira Gershwin who once wrote a jolly song (to music by Kurt Weill) called 'The Cosy Nook Trio' which played pleasingly upon this form of verbal felicity. An Italian Duke, lusting after a painter's model, sings, 'I cannot promise bedding wells.' To which the model replies, 'My thoughts were not on wedding bells.' And neither were his, presumably.

Which brings us to the **FREUDIAN SLIP**, the **SOCIAL CLANGER** and the **DROPPED BRICK**. A Freudian slip is when by seeming to make a mere verbal error we give away our real intentions, as when a host offering to take a female guest's coat says, 'Can I take your clothes off?' I recall a delightful moment several years ago when watching a court-room scene in a musical at the Theatre Royal, Stratford East. The judge was addressing three leggy ladies who were the cause of much distraction in the court. But the actor playing the judge stumbled over his lines and declared roundly (corpsing the cast in the process), 'Stop clittering up the court!'

A number of years ago, an audience of tittering sixth formers (including myself) believed it had encountered another example of this type. We were attending what was known as a Film Appreciation Lecture in the Philharmonic Hall, Liverpool. The speaker was a distinguished director, whose name fortunately I have forgotten, and he was introducing one of his distinguished films. In a throwaway line, he informed us he had just been with Dirk Bogarde in the South of France or somewhere, 'And we've been disgusting together ... er ... discussing ... oh God!'

To these traditional gaffe hunting grounds, the preparation of this book has enabled me to add some splendid examples of the printer's art – **MISPRINTS** or 'literals' as they are known in the trade – and some editorial usage of words which could have done with a sub-editing (but which, fortunately for us, did not get). We do not use these on *Quote ... Unquote* because they must be *seen* to be best appreciated. But here they are now, in living black and white.

While enjoying what sometimes results from the hectic compilation of printed matter, it is only fair to put on the page some classic examples of **BROADCASTING BOOBS** (which are known in the US as **BLOOPERS**). Whether dating back to the formal days of wireless (when the fall from grace was so much further) or from the excessive ad-libbing and informality of today, I felt it was time these magic moments were preserved in a form other than boot-leg recordings. I must apologise if any of the attributions are wrong but I would not lightly pass up some of these gems on a mere technicality.

My own favourite is from the former (and otherwise rather good) Radio 1 disc-jockey, Johnny Walker. Reading out a request he said the listener who had sent it lived in: 'Bury St., Edmunds, Suffolk.' And I really did hear an Irish radio announcer play a record on RTE for a listener who had been – remarkably Ill – a little while before:

'Oh, I'm sorry, he's been *ill* recently. . .'

If only one could recapture in print the full force of some other broadcasting boobs, like the time when William Hardcastle bounced on to *The World at One* and almost said, 'This is William Whitelaw. . .' Or found himself completely incapable of uttering the name 'Herbert Chitepo'.

Another of the Radio Greats in this sphere was Jack de Manio, one-time presenter of *Today*. His speciality was getting the time-checks wrong but I can still recall the *frisson* across the nation's breakfast tables when Jack was back-announcing an interview with a clergyman who had condemned wife-swapping in a parish magazine which just happened to be called 'Cockcrow'. What Jack said was:

'The Revd ———— on what Mr Fletcher MP calls 'our sex-ridden society. And I can't wait to get my cock. . . er. . . my copy of 'Cockcrow'!'

One of the most delicious radio boobs was not, alas, ever broadcast. A too-kind studio manager pointed out to the distinguished academic who was introducing a discussion on aspects of British

Industry that it would be better if he rephrased the words he had used at rehearsal. The academic had planned to introduce the speakers and give their credentials and fields of specialisation, thus:

'Michael Clapham – Director of ICI – chemicals; Val Duncan – Managing Director of Rio Tinto-Zinc – mining; R. D. Young – Deputy Chairman, Alfred Herbert – the Biggest Machine Tool in Europe.'

As with Spoonerisms, **GOLDWYNISMS** attributed to the Master himself are often, if not generally, apocryphal. As Samuel Goldwyn himself once declared, 'Goldwynisms! Don't talk to me about Goldwynisms. Talk to Jesse Lasky!' But the Polish-born film mogul's life-long struggle with the English language deserves a place in a book like this and I have tried to find some lesser-known examples. Incidentally, one wishes that one could have had James Thurber's presence of mind when arguing with Goldwyn over the amount of violence that had crept in to a film treatment of his story *The Secret Life of Walter Mitty*. 'I'm sorry you felt it was too bloody and thirsty,' said Goldwyn. 'Not only did I think so,' replied Thurber, 'I was horror and struck.'

Again, when it comes to **GIELGUDISMS**, one is faced with the question of authenticity. Sir John Gielgud, the great and good actor, is known throughout and beyond the theatrical profession for his dropped bricks. People find him all the more endearing because of this little peccadillo. Indeed, one gets the impression that half the actors in England are hovering by Sir John, waiting for him to let one drop. I have included a tiny sample, one of which at least is absolutely genuine.

The accidental coming together of words is a basic element of humour. A *Quote... Unquote* listener told me of receiving a card on his wedding anniversary which the Post Office had franked with the slogan, 'NOT GETTING ON? Telephone the Marriage Guidance Council.' This was only capped by a colleague who had received a letter from the Race Relations Board franked with the slogan 'KEEP BRITAIN GREEN'.

Notices and signs seem to attract the 'foot in mouth' treatment, especially, as in the battle over lavatories in the House of Lords, following the introduction of women in 1958. The lavatories were originally labelled 'LIFE PEERESSES ONLY' but, as Lady Wootton pointed out, 'We are very passionate that we are not peeresses; peeresses are the wives of peers.' Now the lavatories are marked 'PEERS' and 'WOMEN PEERS'. And so on and so forth. I am most grateful to the numerous people who have contributed tongue-slips and fox's passes to this volume – especially to those who have foregone brain-wipe and admitted to verbal indiscretions of their own. I hope the experience has proved therapeutic. Where possible I have given credit. I apologise for any omissions.

As a writer and broadcaster who occasionally stumbles and who quite frequently commits appalling grammatical errors, I must emphasize that the purpose of this book is not to mock the perpetrators of the gaffes contained herein. I know what it is like to be mocked. Once in the dawn's early light when I was introducing the *Today* programme I ventured to suggest that 'Vanessa Redgrave had to run the gamut of protesters.' It took a mention in the *New Statesman* 'This English' column, a rebuke in a book on the declining standard of English usage, and a trip to the dictionary to make me realise what I had done.

What I hope the gaffes recorded here have in common, however, is not some terrible, ignorant, awfulness but a quality that transcends the grammatical, linguistic or social error upon which they are based – pick-me-ups, in fact, not put-downs.

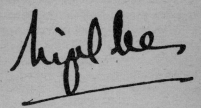

Herbert Marshall
was a British actor who made a name for himself
in Hollywood during the 1930s despite losing a leg
in World War I. He was between marriages when –
or so the story has it – John Gielgud encountered
him with the words:

*'Ah, Herbert, I see you're foot-loose in
Hollywood…'*

Convent
of the
Sisters of Charity

**NO PARKING
NO TURNING**

Walk-out by 150 cripples top hospital

● The Yorkshire Post

Of her son,
taking his finals for an international job, a cousin
of mine said:

*'Of course, if he does well in them, the world's
his lobster.'*

She also said about her daughter-in-law who was
in hospital about to have a Caesarian baby:

*'Nothing to worry about. With a father who's a
top surgeon she's bound to get R.I.P. treatment.'*

A. M. D. CARRIER, LONDON SW7

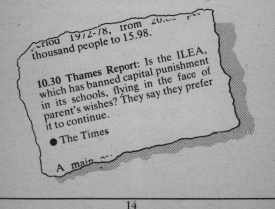

...riod 1972-78, from 20.... p...
thousand people to 15.98.

10.30 Thames Report: Is the ILEA,
which has banned capital punishment
in its schools, flying in the face of
parent's wishes? They say they prefer
it to continue.

● The Times

A main...

At the Wimbledon Championships
Billie Jean King was seen to toss the ball in the air
and observe its movements. Dan Maskell helpfully
explained:

*'Billie Jean has always been conscious of wind
on the centre court.'*

Also at Wimbledon,
a BBC Radio commentator was waxing eloquent
about a South American player:

*'It's remarkable when you consider that in the
whole of Paraguay there are only about two
hundred tennis players. Victor Pecci is one
of those.'*

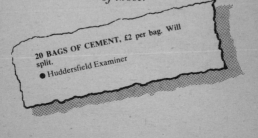

20 BAGS OF CEMENT, £2 per bag. Will
split.
● Huddersfield Examiner

On BBC news
from Norwich there was an item about an open
day at Wisbech sewage farm which included the
following passage:

*'A spokesman for the East Anglian Water
Authority said they considered a trip round the
sewage works a unique and interesting day
out. They were even laying on transport for
people who wanted to go.'*

**THE HITE REPORT ON
MALE SEXUALITY**
September
£12.50 (cased)
£9.95 (limp)

A lady
who used to come to help with the housework was
talking to my sister about her son's
forthcoming marriage:

*'His employers have been very good to him. As
he had no holiday time left they have granted
him passionate leave for his honeymoon.'*

MRS E. F. HOLMES, HOLLAND-ON-SEA

Garage, West Midlands

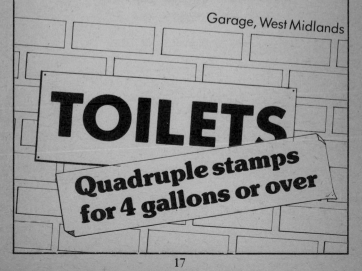

TOILETS

Quadruple stamps
for 4 gallons or over

Educated at Manchester Grammar School, he spoke English with a Lancashire accent, sold his father's German books, reduced the intake of German food and drink, and sent *his* son to Rugby and Roedean.

● Jewish Telegraph

"I know Sir Peter hasn't forgot-

'**A**nd after the news at 9 o'clock, you may like to know that there will be a talk by Sir John MacPherson on "The Land of the Nigger."'

JACK DE MANIO, BBC HOME SERVICE, 29 JANUARY 1956

'**T**hat's the end of the forecast. Now here is the weather.'

RONALD FLETCHER, BBC RADIO

On a visit to Warsaw in December 1978, President Carter told the Poles: 'I have come to learn your opinions and understand your desires for the future.' The American interpreter translated this as:

'I desire the Poles carnally.'

In a reference to the President's departure from Washington, the translation came out:

'When I abandoned the United States, never to return...'

Carter's Press Secretary Jody Powell said: 'It was not a good translation. There will be a new translator tomorrow.'

which includes a light lunch.

Stockport Research Interest Group. Wednesday, January 28, 7pm, School of Nursing. Stepping Hill Hospital. Speaker, Anne Thompson: Why don't women breast feed? Cheese and wine party follows.

● The Nursing Times

WHATEVER the future may hold, it is currently an

I went
to see an old lady and asked how she was:

'Oh dear, I've 'ad an 'orrid shock. My neighbour next door went to one of them parties last night and fell down dead with a trombonis.'

HELEN HIGGS, WIMBORNE

At a luncheon given by Mervyn Hayt, sometime Bishop of Coventry, a nervous curate said to Cosmo Lang, Archbishop of Canterbury:

'Have another piece of Grace, your Cake.'

A married lady
was bemoaning to fellow dinner guests that she
had been extremely naive before her marriage.
To illustrate the extent of her innocence
she remarked:

*'I didn't even know what a homosexual was
until I met my husband.'*

MARY DRURY, PLYMOUTH

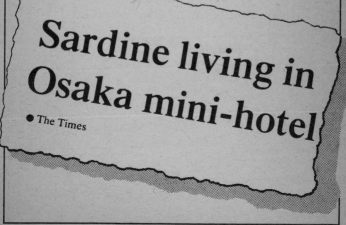

Sardine living in Osaka mini-hotel

● The Times

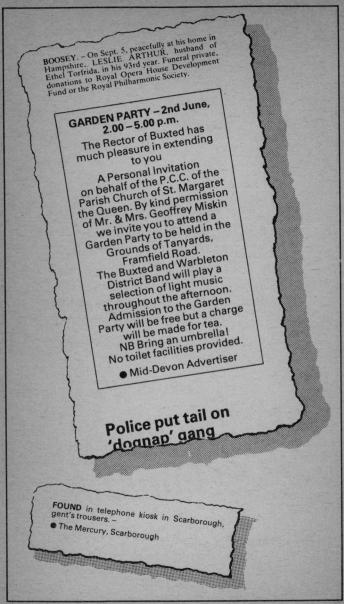

BOOSEY. – On Sept. 5, peacefully at his home in Hampshire, LESLIE ARTHUR, husband of Ethel Torfrida, in his 93rd year. Funeral private, donations to Royal Opera House Development Fund or the Royal Philharmonic Society.

GARDEN PARTY – 2nd June, 2.00 – 5.00 p.m.

The Rector of Buxted has much pleasure in extending to you

A Personal Invitation on behalf of the P.C.C. of the Parish Church of St. Margaret the Queen. By kind permission of Mr. & Mrs. Geoffrey Miskin we invite you to attend a Garden Party to be held in the Grounds of Tanyards, Framfield Road.

The Buxted and Warbleton District Band will play a selection of light music throughout the afternoon. Admission to the Garden Party will be free but a charge will be made for tea. NB Bring an umbrella! No toilet facilities provided.

● Mid-Devon Advertiser

Police put tail on 'dognap' gang

FOUND in telephone kiosk in Scarborough, gent's trousers. –

● The Mercury, Scarborough

In the early days of radio, a leading churchman was conducting a live religious service, conscious that he had to modulate his voice to make it more acceptable for a studio than for a church. After he had concluded the broadcast with the Grace, he commented to the producer: 'I don't think that was too loud, do you?' Unfortunately, this came over the air as:

'... the fellowship of the Holy Ghost, be with us all evermore... I don't think!'

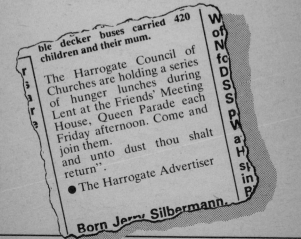

ble decker buses carried 420 children and their mum.

The Harrogate Council of Churches are holding a series of hunger lunches during Lent at the Friends' Meeting House, Queen Parade each Friday afternoon. Come and join them.

and unto dust thou shalt return''.

● The Harrogate Advertiser

Born Jerry Silbermann.

During the 1948 war
in Palestine, the US Ambassador to the United
Nations, Warren Austin, hoped that the Jews and
the Arabs would settle their differences:

'Like good Christians.'

At the wedding
of some friends of mine, instead of saying
'Lawfully joined together' the priest said:

'Joyfully loined together.'

BARBARA REEVE, CHELMSFORD

Mr Latham said: Before
he lectures working peo-
ple on wage claims, he
should look to the
Church's own affairs.
"In my constituency of
Paddington the Church
Commissioners are forc-
ing up rents by several
pounds per wee.

● The Paddington Mer-
cury

one of
a page
ighton

al her

Road,
y the
USA,
Tools

arner
and a
idgid

s of

I was in a play
— *Lord Arthur Savile's Crime*
– and had the line to say, 'Then you should not object to Mr Podgers seeing your palm.' At one performance it came out as:

'Then you should not object to Mr Palmers seeing your podge.'

MISS M. F. DAMESICK, MANCHESTER

SHOP ASSISTANT REQUIRED.

NO OBJECTION TO SEX.

Looe

A former headmaster
of Llandovery College said the following in a
prayer during morning assembly many years ago:

*'Bless us in our intercourse, be it for business
or pleasure.'*

JOHN JENKINS, LLANDOVERY

LUCKY VICTIM WAS STABBED THREE TIMES

● Hackney Gazette

My mother was notoriously bad at remembering names. One year at a seaside boarding house Father suggested she should memorise some everyday word which rhymed with the name she wanted to remember. For a lady whose name was Crummock, Father suggested 'stomach'. Next day as this dignified lady entered the dining room, Mother paused a moment for thought and then chirped happily:

'Good morning, Mrs Kelly!'

SYLVIA TORKINGTON, STOCKPORT

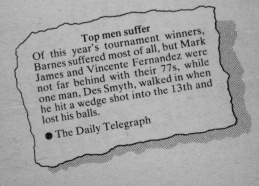

Top men suffer
Of this year's tournament winners, Barnes suffered most of all, but Mark James and Vincente Fernandez were not far behind with their 77s, while one man, Des Smyth, walked in when he hit a wedge shot into the 13th and lost his balls.
● The Daily Telegraph

Patients cut to ease crowding

● Bristol Evening Post

Defender's broken leg hits Haverhill

● Cambridge Evening News

M y elderly

aunt told me she had been to see the play:

'Arsenal and Old lace'

MRS A. ALEXANDER, NEWCASTLE-UPON-TYNE

'M r *Thorpe insisted*

that he hadn't known Andrew Newton before he
went to goal, hadn't seen him while he was in
goal, and had had no contact with him since
being released from goal.'

ITN REPORTER

nave done some years ago.

After the Hungarian uprising of
1956, Kocsis moved to Switzerland
and layed for Young Fellows. Subsequently, he signed for Barcelona.

● The Daily Telegraph

The mixed saunas will be held
two days a week.
City council leader the Day Ken

29

Dan Maskell was providing the commentary for TV coverage of a Braniff Airways Mens Doubles tennis match in which David Lloyd and Mark Cox were participating. At one point he remarked:

'The British boys are now adopting the attacking position — Cox up.'

CONVENIENCES
CYCLISTS DISMOUNT

Southgate

The old tea-clipper *Cutty Sark* was being installed for public inspection in a dry dock beside the River Thames at Greenwich. In front of Prince Philip, sundry other distinguished guests and the serried ranks of the media, the Mayor of Greenwich proudly referred to the vessel as:

'The Sutty Cark.'

My favourite spoonerism
was alleged to have been originated by the Station
Commander at an RAF station in the Canal Zone
round about 1952 when I was there. At church
parade the order was given:

'Roam out the fallen Catholics!'

JACK EVANS, WIMBORNE

I collected my Grandmother
(aged 78) from a Christmas party where everyone
had supplied a dish. She got in the car and
announced that her stomach was giving her jip.
When asked why, she replied:

'Well, dear, I had chicken in Harpic.'

GILLIAN PARKER, MOULTON

Three fall down hole in shop

Three people were taken to hospital
yesterday after a 12ft hole opened up
under them in the Quick Turnover
Fruiterers in Gillingham High Street,
Kent.

● The Sunday Express

Arrangements had been made for us
to meet up with another couple to go out together.
My wife who was dressed up to the nines blurted
out, 'We thought you'd get dressed up.' There was
an awkward silence and then one of them
replied dismally:

'We thought we had.'

PETER NELSON, HULL

DEPRESSED MAN DIED ON RAILWAY LINE

TWENTY GOLDEN GOLDWYNISMS

1 'We can get
all the Indians we need at the reservoir.'

2 'Too caustic?
To hell with the cost, we'll make the picture
anyway.'

3 'It's spreading like wildflowers!'

4 'I want
you to make a bust of my wife's hands.'

5 'I read part
of the book right the way through.'

6 'You ought to take
the bull between the teeth.'

7 'Anyone who goes
to a psychiatrist needs to have his head
examined.'

8 'I'll give you a definite maybe.'

9 'First you have a good story, then a good treatment, and next a first-rate director. After that you hire a competent cast and even then you have only the mucus of a good picture.'

10 'Let's have some new cliches.'

11 'This makes me so sore, it gets my dandruff up.'

12 'The A-Bomb – that's dynamite!'

13 'Lets bring it up to date with some snappy nineteenth century dialogue.'

14 'I'd like to propose a toast to Marshall Field Montgomery Ward.'

15 'Tell me, how did you love the picture?'

16 'I don't remember where I got this new Picasso. In Paris, I think. Somewhere over there on the Left Wing.'

17 'That's my Toujours Lautrec.'

18 'You just don't realise what life is all about until you have found yourself lying on the brink of a great abscess.'

19 'This is written in blank werse.'

20 'I want you to be sure and see my Hans Christian Anderson. It's full of charmth and warmth.'

It happened soon after
the last war when many civilians were still wearing
Utility Clothing. My husband had to change trains
at Basingstoke and went into the Tea Room for a
cup of tea. A couple entered. The man was
wearing an almost identical hat and coat and
carried a very similar week-end case to my
husband's. They sat at the next table. The man
opened his newspaper and the woman went to the
tea counter. A few minutes later the woman put the
tray of tea and biscuits on the table and whispered
into my husband's ear:

*'Shan't be long, darling. I'm just going to
the doings.'*

HILDA F. READ, BARKING

Heard in the sermon
at a marriage – the priest holy, innocent and
slightly dotty, said:

*'Sometimes in a marriage, the couple have
been known to get on top of each other…'*

REVD. B. PAUL GILROY, EWLOE

LESSON CHANGE TIME
IF THERE IS A FIRE ALARM
AT THIS TIME, THE WHOLE
SCHOOL WILL IMMEDIATELY
EVACUATE, AND
ASSEMBLE ON THE FIELD.

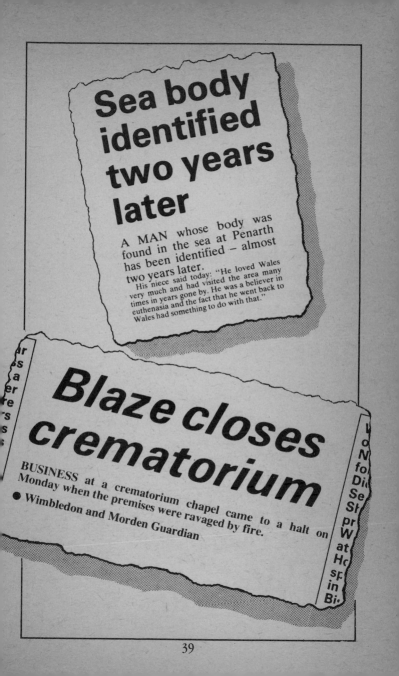

Sea body identified two years later

A MAN whose body was found in the sea at Penarth has been identified – almost two years later.

His niece said today: "He loved Wales very much and had visited the area many times in years gone by. He was a believer in euthanasia and the fact that he went back to Wales had something to do with that."

Blaze closes crematorium

BUSINESS at a crematorium chapel came to a halt on Monday when the premises were ravaged by fire.

● Wimbledon and Morden Guardian

Ðuring a disagreeable discussion
on dogs, my mother-in-law made the following
observation:

*'Well, I think some dogs ought to be
compulsorily castrated. They shouldn't be
allowed to increase willy-nilly.'*

P. BRANTLEY, HARLINGTON

deliver work.

● Forest of Dean Guardian

Asked why the books show
£50,000 owed in arrears,
deputy housing manager
Wilf Pickett told the housing
committee that nearly half
the figure was accountable to
former tenants. "These are
people who have died without giving us notice," he
explained.

● St Albans and Harpenden
Review

Vandals

mp-
col-
res-
wift
hot.
the
ols
are
cle
ed
lso
use
ce A
e is

SIK
some
tidy t
H
appe
The
wee
grov
flots
The
slop
yea
W
pon
bur

Young boy in Regent's Park:

'What's that funny building, Nan?'

Nan:

*'It's where the Government sends foreigners to
say their prayers. It's called a kiosk.'*

RITA CANAVAN, SOUTHEND-ON-SEA

First Female Relative:
*'When I was on holiday in Spain, I nearly got
stung by those huge jellyfish.'*

Second Female Relative:
'You mean the Portuguese Menopause?'

R. N. W. ELLIS, LLANGAMMACH WELLS

Gone are the days of senior boys flogging their juniors,
while capital punishment by staff is undertaken to a much
lesser degree than previously.
● The Stafford Newsletter

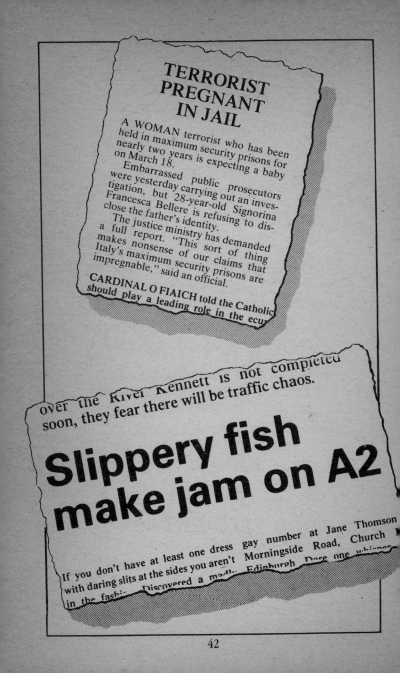

TERRORIST PREGNANT IN JAIL

A WOMAN terrorist who has been held in maximum security prisons for nearly two years is expecting a baby on March 18.

Embarrassed public prosecutors were yesterday carrying out an investigation, but 28-year-old Signorina Francesca Bellere is refusing to disclose the father's identity.

The justice ministry has demanded a full report. "This sort of thing makes nonsense of our claims that Italy's maximum security prisons are impregnable," said an official.

CARDINAL O FIAICH told the Catholic should play a leading role in the ecu

over the River Kennett is not completed soon, they fear there will be traffic chaos.

Slippery fish make jam on A2

If you don't have at least one dress with daring slits at the sides you aren't in the fashi Discovered a madl

gay number at Jane Thomson Morningside Road, Church Edinburgh Dore one whisper

STROKE PATIENTS DON'T FEEL ALONE

Doctor's waiting room, Colchester

During the riots in Chicago during the 1968 Democratic Convention, Mayor Richard J. Daley addressed the press:

'Gentlemen, get the thing straight once and for all.
The policeman isn't there to create disorder, the policeman is there to preserve disorder.'

Joint body plan for cemetery

● The Hereford Times

German food and drink, and sent ...
son to Rugby and Roedean.

She added that she didn't know
where the couple were heading
for their honeymoon. "I think he
was going to surprise her with
something," she said.

● The Western Telegraph

From 1928 to 1949,
'Uncle Don' – Don Carney – was the host of a
popular children's show on radio station WOR,
broadcast over a large part of the United States. He
spent his life trying to deny that he had ever let slip
one of the most famous clangers of all when,
thinking he was off the air, he said:

'I guess that'll hold the little bastards.'

GET YOUR MILKMAN TO LAY ON SOME EGGS

'**D**ear Miss, Sorry Jimmy is late but me and my husband rather overdone it this morning.'

'**D**ear Miss, Please excuse Mary from having a shower, being how she is. Being how you are yourself sometimes, you will understand how she is.'

Top-hated Bishop stole the show at fete

● The Salisbury Journal

Welbeck Stables

SINGLE GIRL GROOM

required
to work under stud
groom.
Able to ride/exercise.

'**P**rincess Margaret, wearing an off-the-hat
face…'

MAX ROBERTSON, BBC RADIO

'**F**loods
of molten lager, flowing down the
mountainside.'

STUART HIBBERD, BBC RADIO

prime steak 7 OZ. £2.50 per lb £1.57

Direct from the seat of the
Earl of Harewood

PRIME RUMP STEAK

Keighley

During the 1979 Cricket World Cup
when England was playing Canada, BBC radio
commentator Christopher Martin-Jenkins drew
attention to the inclement conditions under which
the match was being played:

*'It is extremely cold here. The England fielders
are keeping their hands in their pockets
between balls.'*

At the 1980
Democratic Party Convention in New York, prior
to his ignominious defeat by Ronald Reagan in the
Presidential Election, Jimmy Carter accepted his
party's renomination as candidate by referring to
some of the great Democrats who had never made
it to the White House. In particular he mentioned:

*'The Great President who might have been –
Hubert Horatio Hornblower.'*

A dear old great aunt
of mine died when I was about thirteen. The
grown-ups were discussing her – how she had
been a patient little woman with a bullying
husband. One was so carried away she
announced:

*'There's no doubt about it, he prolonged the
shortening of her days.'*

MRS C. E. MARTIN, NEW ROMNEY

AT
SHAFTESBURY TOWN HALL (GUILDHALL)
ON:–

Tuesday 11th. July at 8 p.m. Come and see:

–"The Final Hour" followed by tea & buscuits.

Many years ago
the then Lord Altrincham came to the local
Grammar school at Chipping Sodbury to present
the prizes. In the introductory speech, a local
councillor began:

*'How pleased we are that Our Lord has come
down…'*

MRS D. J. BROCK, BRISTOL

with gold insets of nude women, and it is about eight inches wide at the wildest point.

TOILETS ARE NOT NECESSARY

Ladies who like a flutter at the bookies won't be able to spend a penny – for bookmakers don't have to provide toilet facilities of any kind.

This was revealed to members of Dumbarton District Licensing Board.

At the previous meeting members were told that a gents toilet was available but no ladies loo – and they had heard rumblings from female customers.

● Helensburgh Advertiser

My 'chat show' — by the reggae riot Pc

SID SCOTT made his stage debut at a reggae concert ... and stopped a riot.

As 'souffles' broke out in the huge crowd, he told the fans:

'This is nothing to do with you or the police. It's just an unfortunate incident.

● The Daily Star

A GREEK urn worth £200 was stolen from St Osyth Priory on Tues-

high, with two purple handles edged in gold.

Largest ever heroine haul

● The Newcastle Journal

A WOMAN held in max nearly two on March 1…

'**A**t Oxford Crown Court today,
Donald Neilsen denied being the Pink Panther.'

EDWARD COLE, RADIO 4

I am a Lay Reader.
When taking evensong soon after my licencing I
called on the congregation to:

'Come with me unto the Groan of Thrace.'

BRYAN OWEN, DEAL

Vandals are kept at bay

CHARITY workers are combatting vandalism at a Hove church hall with a live-in warden.

Last year a glass door was smashed, fire extinguishers were let off, floors were damaged by cyclists and roller skaters and people were using the lavatories as public conveniences.

● Brighton and Hove Leader

Traffic will hit homes if motorway is scrapped

● The Sutton Herald

A while ago, a friend of mine,
who is a policeman, had occasion to stop a car
and speak to its driver. The driver did not take
kindly to being held up in this way and was being
rather abrupt and unhelpful. His wife, who was in
the car with him, felt obliged to try and calm down
the situation before her husband got himself into
trouble, so she leaned over and said to
the policeman:

*'Please don't pay too much heed to him. He's
always like this when he's had a few.'*

ALISTAIR EDWARDS, WILSMLOW

Geisha Night Club

At the 12th floor overlooking a Magnificent, Scintillating view of Cairo by Night is the "GEISHA" A Dance Band and an Oriental Dancer creating an Atmosphere of "A Thousand and one Nights" dont miss it . . ,

Take the Elevator and Press the 12th Bottom
NOW !

For your Diner we sugest . . .

    " l'Entrecote GEISHA "

● Atlas Hotel, Cairo

My wife and I were setting off
on our honeymoon late in the evening, and an
aged relative, on hearing that we had quite a
distance to travel, inquired:

'Are you going all the way tonight?'

MATTHEW COCHRANE, MAGHULL

Sir John Gielgud was being interviewed
late at night on a local television show in St Louis,
Missouri. Peter Ustinov, who just happened to be
there watching it go out, recalls how Sir John was
asked who had been the greatest influence on his
early career. Sir John replied:

*'Claude Rains. But I don't know what happened
to him afterwards. I think he failed and went to
America.'*

Sir John told the theatre director Patrick Garland that he was going down to Chichester to do a play with Robin Phillips whom he did not know. 'I hear he's very young,' commented Sir John. 'I know him very well,' replied Garland. 'He's about my age.' To which the Gielgudism was:

'Oh, he's not so young then.'

broken leg

CARDINAL O FIAICH told the Catholic clergy yesterday that they should play a leading role in the ecumenical movement and he made three suggestions as to how they could play out that role. He suggested that in offering prayers for persons recently deceased they include prayers for members of the local Protestant community who had died. He further suggested that Protestants be included in the priests' prayers for the sick.

● Cork Examiner

Worried Ousden residents are praying for
b... over troubled waters. If work on

We were passing through the village where Gray's *Elegy* was written when a lady at the rear of the bus remarked to her companion:

'I have always wanted to go to Poke Stoges.'

NANCY REDFERN, CAMBRIDGE

'*People behind Martina Navratilova on the roller, have the best view of her receiving service.'*

MAX ROBERTSON, BBC RADIO

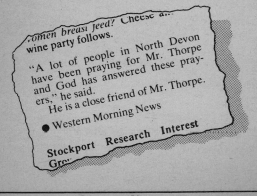

...omen breast feed? Cheese a...
wine party follows.

"A lot of people in North Devon have been praying for Mr. Thorpe and God has answered these prayers," he said.

He is a close friend of Mr. Thorpe.

● Western Morning News

Stockport Research Interest Gro...

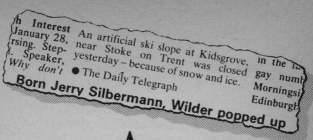

Ample,
rosy-faced lady with bulging shopping bag on bus:

*'Yerse, she took up wiv one of them
new-fangled religions. You know, the Seven Day
Adventuresses.'*

CONSTANCE DARG, TONBRIDGE

At a Labour
committee meeting in the Midlands, the
Chairman, in his opening remarks, was heard
to say:

*'Brothers, as you all know, certain allegations
have been made against me. I will reply to these
at the next meeting after I have confronted the
alligators.'*

ERIC A. BIRCH, ILFORD

THIS IS THE
BRITISH BROADCORPING
CASTRATION

Golden Moments
from the Wireless — the
perpetrators of which remain,
happily, anonymous:

❝There is the danger of civil war
if the Kurds don't get their way.**❞**

❝A series of strikes
at the Liverpool Royal Hospital has caused
a lot of ill feeling.**❞**

❝There is a
trough of low pleasure over Europe.**❞**

❝We are now to hear
some Birdsong by Plain.**❞**

❝Police fired
rubber bullocks . . . er, sorry, bullets.**❞**

❝ Widespread fist and mog can be expected. **❞**

❝ There will be no sun
today because of an industrial dispute. **❞**

❝ And now a record dedication
for Mrs Ethel Smith who is one hundred
years old today. But I'm told she's dead
with-it. **❞**

❝ Aristotle Onassis,
the Greek shitting typoon. **❞**

❝ We shall now hear Bolero's Ravel. **❞**

❝ The trouble has been caused by
unpatriotic elephants in the country. **❞**

❝ In winter bullfinches
are best fed on bacon rinds and great tits
like coconuts. **❞**

❝More about that delay
on British Rail Southern Region. We have
our reporter on the line...**❞**

❝As a result of the strike
by Aer Lingus staff, anyone wishing to fly to
Birmingham will have to go by boat.**❞**

❝There has been a heavy fall of rain
here at Trent Bridge but fortunately it didn't
touch the ground.**❞**

❝And now we have
the Bathroom Orchestra from Pump.**❞**

❝The unorganised conference... er,
I'm sorry, the U.N. organised conference...**❞**

❝Reports are coming in
from Australia that Serbo Croat extremists
have attempted to sabotage the Sydney
water supply by *blowing* up the *pipes.***❞**

And
two bloopers from American radio:

'We'll be right back after this word from General Fools.'

'This portion of <u>Woman on the Run</u> is brought to you by Phillips' Milk of Magnesia.'

PLEASE DO NOT LOCK THE DOOR AS WE HAVE LOST THE KEY

hotel Ireland

'**T**here's Neil Harvey
*at leg slip with his legs wide apart, waiting for
a tickle.'*

BRIAN JOHNSTON, BBC RADIO

This was only topped
by Brian Johnston commentating on the Oval Test
against the West Indies in 1976 with Michael
Holding bowling to Peter Willey:

'The bowler's Holding, the batsman's Willey.'

In Nottingham, travel agents believe the threats will result in few cancellations of holidays.

Mr. Tony Whittall, manager at Fairville Travel in Clumber Street, commented: "It's going on every day in Belfast. I don't think bombs have the same sort of 'feel' about them that they might have done some years ago."

● Nottingham Evening Post

64

Lorry driver John Hey
Mellor was found guilty of
carless driving and was fined
£150 with £51.30 costs.
● The Yorkshire Evening
Post

On another occasion Trevor Bailey
had been singing the praises of Peter Willey when
he suddenly produced this remarkable admission:

'I am, of course, a great Willey supporter.'

Brothers fell foul of law

TWO Ballygawley brothers fell
foul of the law when they were
caught by the police for two
motoring offences.

They were Dennis Gillespie, an
18-year-old chicken catcher, and
his 25-year-old brother, George, a
hen catcher.

● Stabone Weekly News

At a conference in Berlin
in 1954, the French Foreign Minister, Georges
Bidault, was hailed as:

'That fine little French tiger, Georges Bidet.'

At one time a certain pop star
was famous for splitting his pants during
performances. An elderly lady with whom I
worked burst into the office and said breathlessly:

*'Did you hear about J. B. Priestley splitting his
trousers on stage?'*

MRS C. WHEELER, LONDON E.3

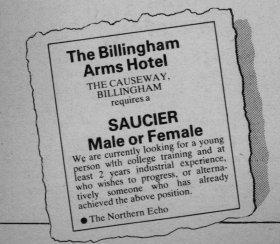

The Billingham
Arms Hotel

THE CAUSEWAY,
BILLINGHAM
requires a

SAUCIER
Male or Female

We are currently looking for a young
person with college training and at
least 2 years industrial experience,
who wishes to progress, or alterna-
tively someone who has already
achieved the above position.

● The Northern Echo

O_{n a wet day}
on holiday in France we borrowed a Scrabble set
from a French family. Later at a cocktail party in
England I was explaining to two friends how
difficult it is playing in English with two many QU's
and C's etc. In one of those terrible lulls in
conversation my voice rang across the room:

*'You've no idea how tiresome it is trying to play
Scrabble with French letters.'*

TONY ROUNSEFELL, CHELTENHAM

Gierek political eclipse

Mr Edward Gierek, the former Pol-
ish Communist Party leader, and
seven of his closet associates resigned
their parliamentary seats, completing
their political eclipse.

● The Times

The justice ministry has demanded
a full report. "This sort of thing
makes nonsense of our claims that
Italy's maximum security prisons are
impregnable," said an official.

Peter West – again – talking about the seeding of Jimmy Connors at Wimbledon:

'Connors' wife is expecting a baby and there was some doubt about his entry.'

'Miss Stove *seems to have gone off the boil.'*

PETER WEST, BBC RADIO

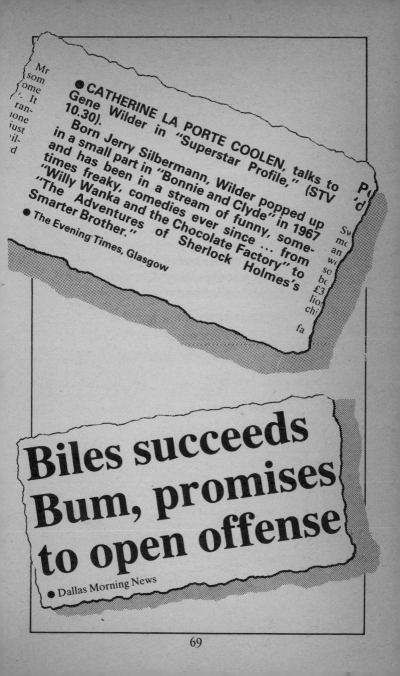

● CATHERINE LA PORTE COOLEN, talks to Gene Wilder in "Superstar Profile," (STV 10.30).

Born Jerry Silbermann, Wilder popped up in a small part in "Bonnie and Clyde" in 1967 and has been in a stream of funny, sometimes freaky, comedies ever since ... from "Willy Wanka and the Chocolate Factory" to "The Adventures of Sherlock Holmes's Smarter Brother."

● The Evening Times, Glasgow

Biles succeeds Bum, promises to open offense

● Dallas Morning News

My dear Norwegian mother
spoke quite fluent English but occasionally
became a little confused over proverbs. Her best
effort, I think, was when she reprimanded me for
being ungrateful about a present I had received:

*'Never, never, cast your teeth in a
gift-horse's face!'*

MRS E. S. B. PASHLEY, COTTINGHAM

President Richard M. Nixon once said:

'Scrubbing floors and emptying bedpans has as much dignity as the Presidency.'

President Gerald R. Ford declared:

'Whenever I can I always watch the Detroit Tigers on radio.'

PRESS

I had entered the wrong time
in my diary for a Harvest Festival Supper at my
church and consequently arrived an hour late.
Wanting to apologise in a light-hearted way, I
heard myself say:

*'Ladies and gentlemen, I cannot remember ever
being late for such a function as a Harvest
Supper before, but it seems that tonight I have
well and truly clotted my bottybook...'*

REVD JOHN E. BOURNE, STROUD

For not one single bottle
gets the Löwenbräu label
until the brew has been
tasted and passed by a
panel of German beer
experts. Who have rigidly
Teutonic standards when it
comes to beer. (Amongst
other things).

A crony at work
told me a friend of his was up before the bench:

'For living on the immortal earnings of his wife.'

JOHN TAYLOR, NOTTINGHAM

'The time
is twenty-half and a five minutes past eight.'

TOM CROWE, RADIO 3

Fiona draws them in

SEX queen Fiona Richmond had promised to auction her knickers to raise cash for the children, but she had to let them down on the day.

● The Mercury

SAUCIER

Children-for-sale row

By OUR ATHENS CORRESPONDENT

A FURTHER inquiry into a couple on the Aegean island of Lesbos who have been producing children for sale to wealthy childless couples, has been ordered following protests from Greek women's lib organisations.

The protests are on the grounds that the mother is "the victim of the most extreme form of male exploration."

● The Daily Telegraph

While our scripture teacher
was telling us the story of one of the miracles, my
friend was surreptitiously toasting her toes on the
radiator. The teacher said:

*'Jesus walked on the water — and that, Jean
Morrison, is just the way to get chilblains.'*

MAUREEN THRELFALL, PRESTON

In Australia there is a deadly insect
called a Funnel Web spider. A newscaster is
reported to have announced:

*'This afternoon in Sydney a woman was bitten
on the funnel by a finger-web spider.'*

Bridgnorth Athletic Club has
folded because of lack of support by
athletes.

Mr Stuart Williams, who had been
running the club single-handed, said:
"There is a complete lack of apathy
in Bridgnorth. I am very sad about
what has happened."

● Bridgnorth Journal

My mother
was having a cataract operation and the lady in the
next bed told her that she was suffering from a:

'Detached retinue.'

JANE BAKER, THAME

Ed Stewart was introducing records
on his Radio 2 show and had been asked to play a
romantic record for an old lady celebrating her
89th birthday. He said:

'It's entitled, "Until it's time for you to go."'

CHEESE AND PICKLE 75p
HAM AND TOMATO 80p
_____

No increase in prices due to V.A.T. while stocks last.

On list of British Rail sandwich prices after V.A.T. increase one. The smallest weer not used to wearing knickers.

Quiet village

The village of Lingdale was quiet today after the annual exodus to Scarborough on the outing arranged by the village working men's club. Eleven double decker buses carried 420 children and their mum.

● **Middlesborough Evening Gazette**

"The little children are more utgoing than the adults. They have all made

---

The new South African Ambassador to Uruguay, Mr E J. Fourie, told his first press conference in Montivideo, in May 1981:

'I am very happy to be in Peru.'

Jack de Manio was interviewing a newly appointed woman assistant governor at a man's prison. He asked her:

'Do you think the prisoners will regard you as a good screw?'

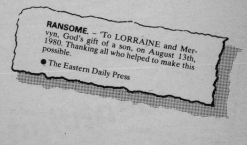

RANSOME. – 'To LORRAINE and Mervyn, God's gift of a son, on August 13th, 1980. Thanking all who helped to make this possible.

● The Eastern Daily Press

BRIGHTON'S Jane Warner is one of the country's top models, a page three pin-up, former Miss Brighton and magazine cover girl.

But this week we can reveal her latest title.

Miss Warner, 19, of Ryde Road, Brighton, has been chosen by the Ridge Tool company of Ohio, USA, to be their Miss Ridgid Tools 1979/80.

As winner of the title, Miss Warner got a free trip to America and a special bonus – a gold plated Ridgid Tool.

It was one of the little perks of my job."

● Brighton and Hove Gazette and Herald

Pregnant woman acquitted

A PREGNANT woman was acquitted by the Nicosia District Court yesterday for violating the weekend motoring regulations by using her car to see her doctor.

Defence counsel Mr Michalakis Papapetrou told the court that the accused, Erini Eleftheriadou, of Pallouriotissa, was in the last month of her pregnancy and she went on Sunday to consult Dr Angelis at his clinic.

Counsel presented to the court a certificate from Dr Angelis verifying the visit.

The court acquitted her under the reservation that she does not repeat the offence within nine months.

● Cyprus Mail

identified

son to Rugby and Roedean.

Winners: Walking Troupes, 1 New Treasure Club, 2 Hawley Grasshoppers, 3 North-West Kent Club for the Dead; **Bands**, 1 Belvedere Drum Majorettes 2.
● The Kentish Times

TERRORIST

Shortly after the engagement had been announced between Prince Charles and Lady Diana Spencer, the Prince attended a luncheon of industrialists and civic heads in Glasgow. Mr Peter Balfour, a leading Scottish businessman, no doubt conversant with the names of many girls previously associated with the Prince, proposed a toast wishing him long life and conjugal happiness with:

'*. . . Lady Jane.*'

ʃrina
o dis-

nded
thing
that

FULL LENGTH undertakers coat, left shoulder slightly worn, £6 —
● The Chester Observer

A bibulous guest at a Foreign Office
reception waltzed up to another guest and trilled,
'Lovely creature in scarlet – dance with me!'
The object of this request replied:

*'I am the Apostolic delegate and I don't think
you're in any condition to dance with me.'*

A ngela Rippon in a BBC Television
news broadcast referred to a Government decision
to draw up:

'Gay puide-lines.'

Are your cook's drawers really good enough?

JUST go into the kitchen and make a swift
check of the cook's drawers. Are they really the
sort of thing you want around your food while
it is being prepared? Can you remove them
easily? Could you wash them, or even wipe
them clean without a lot of frustration?

When it was discovered
that the Stone of Scone had been taken from
under the Coronation Chair in Westminster Abbey
(Scottish nationalists were responsible), the news
was handed to Lionel Marson as he read the Six
O'Clock bulletin on 25 December 1950. He
concluded the item by saying:

*'The Stone of Scone was first brought to
England in 1297 by Edward Isst.'*

When subsequently challenged, he replied that as
the news had been handed to him while he was on
the air, he had not had a chance to think about it.
'I realise now, of course, that I should have said
Edward Iced.'

CORDE ARMONICHE

STRINGS - SAITEN

CORDES - CUERDAS

Dogal

V 21

VIOLINO

MARCHIO VERDE
LAMINATA

A or
2nd

Thanks to this type of metal strings, it has been possible to achieve both the switness of sound and the softness, to feel that, one can recall the bowel strings of the past, but this type far better than the latter owing to the promptness in emission and the ready and stable tuning.

My schoolteacher niece in New Zealand
gave her class of ten-year-olds a list of words
which were to be used, one at a time, in a short
passage to demonstrate their exact meaning. One
word was 'Frugal' which one boy clearly knew had
something to do with saving. He wrote:

*'A beautiful princess was at the top of a tall
tower. She saw a handsome prince riding by.
"Frugal me, frugal me," cried the beautiful
princess. So the handsome prince climbed the
tall tower and he frugalled her and they lived
happily ever after.'*

CHRISTINE BURDEKIN, TRURO

Noel Coward

took part in a television interview on his 70th
birthday. Admitting to a lack of formal education
he said:

*'I learnt all I know at Twickenham Public
Lavatory... er... Library.'*

A commentator on the

400 metres heats at the 1976 Olympic Games in
Montreal asserted:

*'Juantorena opens wide his legs and shows
his class.'*

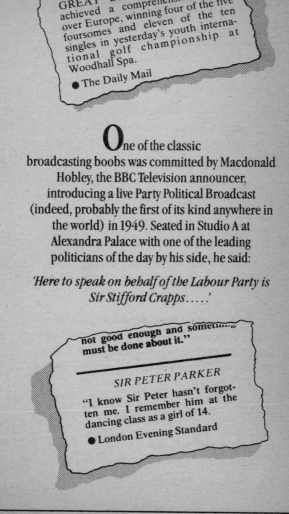

Youth triumph

GREAT BRITAIN and Ireland achieved a comprehensive victory over Europe, winning four of the five foursomes and eleven of the ten singles in yesterday's youth international golf championship at Woodhall Spa.

● The Daily Mail

One of the classic broadcasting boobs was committed by Macdonald Hobley, the BBC Television announcer, introducing a live Party Political Broadcast (indeed, probably the first of its kind anywhere in the world) in 1949. Seated in Studio A at Alexandra Palace with one of the leading politicians of the day by his side, he said:

'Here to speak on behalf of the Labour Party is Sir Stifford Crapps . . . . .'

not good enough and something must be done about it."

SIR PETER PARKER

"I know Sir Peter hasn't forgotten me. I remember him at the dancing class as a girl of 14.

● London Evening Standard

TWENTY CHOICE SCHOOLBOY HOWLERS

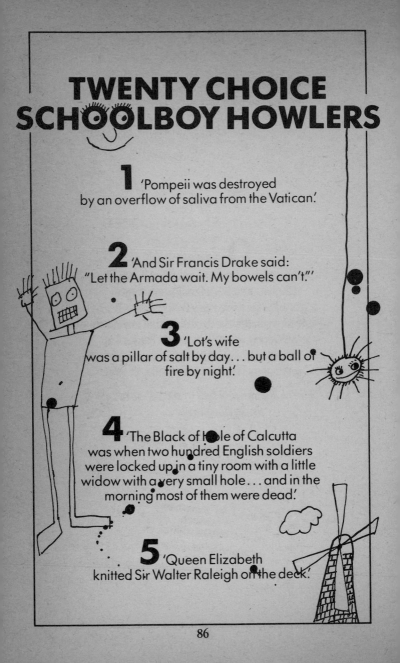

1 'Pompeii was destroyed by an overflow of saliva from the Vatican.'

2 'And Sir Francis Drake said: "Let the Armada wait. My bowels can't."'

3 'Lot's wife was a pillar of salt by day... but a ball of fire by night.'

4 'The Black of Hole of Calcutta was when two hundred English soldiers were locked up in a tiny room with a little widow with a very small hole... and in the morning most of them were dead.'

5 'Queen Elizabeth knitted Sir Walter Raleigh on the deck.'

6 'When Mary heard she was to be the mother of Jesus, she went off and sang the *Magna Carta*.'

7 'Our Lady and all the angels have lilos over their heads.'

8 'Christopher Columbus circumcised the world with forty foot clippers.'

9 'A kangaroo keeps its baby in the porch.'

10 'Last weekend, the Bishop came to our school and turned some of the Sisters into Mothers in a short, but interesting, ceremony.'

11 'The Romans did not conquer Whales because they did not understand what the welsh were saying.'

12 'Henry VIII always had difficulty getting Catherine of Aragon pregnant.'

13 'Henry VIII's wives – Chattering of Argon, Amber Lin, Jane Saymore, Ann of Cloves, Catherine Purr.'

14 'The Pope was inflammable.'

15 'Viking ships could sail up rivers because they had hoars.'

16 'Suffragettes were things the Germans shot under water to kill the British in the First World War.'

17 'I know that my reindeer liveth.'

18 'A cuckoo is a bird which lays other birds' eggs in its own nest, and *viva voce*.'

19 'An orchestra has a man called a conductor who stands out in front with a piece of paper which tells him what music the orchestra is playing.'

20 'Macbeth's courage failed him at the last minuet.'

I was a District Nursing Sister
and was attending a parents 'do' at my son's
school. A strange gentleman came across to me
through the crowd greeting me like an old friend,
saying, 'You remember me, you came when I was
out of hospital with a fractured leg.' Light dawned
and I replied rather loudly during a lull in
the hubbub:

*'Oh, of course I know you. I'm so sorry, I would
only know you in bed.'*

RUTH GALE, HINCKLEY

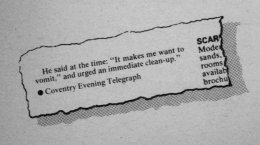

In a coffee shop one morning, my mother and I heard a piercing female voice (belonging to my doctor's wife) cut through the gentle murmur, 'Every time I go into the garden I take off ten years.' This was followed by an embarrassing little silence filled by my mother's remark:

'She ought to stay out there.'

SUZANNE WILLIAMSON, BEXHILL-ON-SEA

Mr Charles Vaggers, once Mr Thorpe's staunchest political ally and his local chairman until last March, said: "There is relief and euphoria today, and the red carpet will be rolled out if Mr Thorpe comes to Barnstaple. But questions remain in people's minds. A lot of queer things have been happening."

● The Sunday Express

The event was a nativity play
and the Angel Gabriel announced his presence to
the Virgin Mary with the words:

'Hail! Thou that art highly-flavoured...'

ANGELA HOYLE, HALIFAX

'**A** *passing policeman*
was unable to revive Mr X despite using the kiss
of death.'

ROBIN HOLMES, RADIO 4

The Lockheed Corporation was fined $647,000 (£312,500) in Washington yesterday after admitting paying out brides to Japanese officials, most of them earmarked for the office of former Prime Minister, Mr Kakuei Tanaka.

● The Daily Telegraph

Our concierge will be happy to supply you with stamps, post-cards and any information you may require.We would ask you to contact the concierge immediately if you should have any problem regarding the hotel and its services, so that we are able to do all possible to give you complete satisfaction, and make stay a happy one. Please don't wait last minutes then it will be too late to arrange any inconveniences.

● Hotel Carand, Sourento

The actor Peter Jones had just started to appear in the TV series 'Mr Big' when he was accosted by a lady in the street:

'Oh, Mr Jones, I do so enjoy your programme. It's so <u>mediocre</u> – something in it for the whole family.'

David Coleman described Asa Hartford, the footballer at one time thought to have a hole in the heart, as:

'A whole-hearted player.'

SYNOPSIS

ACT ONE

A small pizza in Venice

It is the day of the Duke of Urbino's masked ball and his valet tells the café-owner, Pappacoda, that his master wants to meet Barbara again – the masked girl whom he met last year.

● Theatre programme, Manchester

Notes on the

stable fragrance which lasts
throughout the day.

If you don't have at least one dress
with daring slits at the sides you aren't
in the fashion. Discovered a madly
gay number at Jane Thomson at
Morningside Road, Church Hill,
Edinburgh. Dare one whisper it is
worn bra-less, but discreetly placed
pockets serve a useful purpose.

● The Scotsman

It was the classic kidnap. Mr
Sweeney was to take the ransom
money to a phone box near his home

My husband is a Minister
much prone to gaffes. When a guest at a wedding
reception told him that Mr So-and-So was in
hospital for an operation on his piles, my husband
commented:

*'Poor man, he <u>has</u> had a rough passage
this year.'*

MRS J. EVANS, BRADFORD

CONSIGNMENT RECEIVED IN GOOD CONDITION

DRIVERS SIGNATURE

IDENTIFYIN
ARE AFFIXEL
AND ON EAC
YOUR CONSI

RECEIVERS SIGNATURE_____ TIME_____

PRINT NAME_____ DATE_____

GALLONAGE CERTIFICATES — These forms should be completed in LITRES.

● Milk Marketing Board instruction

Rising costs hit jewellers balls

● Retail Jeweller

CARDINAL O FIAICH told the Catholic clergy yeste____ that they should play a leading role in the ecumenical ____ and he

LEAMINGTON-based Automotive Products, the vehicle component manufacturers, are on target for a record-breaking year in the export market.

"We have never been more optimistic about our future," said managing director Mr George Pears.

"We are now seeing the benefits of our long-term strategy to develop well-balanced business and diversify into new mistakes," he said.

● Birmingham Evening Mail

From the BBC 2
commentary on a doubles game at
. Wimbledon, 1980:

*'He doesn't miss many like that, Brian
Gottfried. He practises assiduously. He's the
only married man on court.'*

Received directly, face-to-face,
in conversation with a friend some years ago:

*'Ah, poor soul, she's got something eternal, you
know. She's got a cyst on her aviary.'*

DOROTHY MAIR, BRIGHTON

During World War Two King Haakon of Norway was in exile in London and from time to time made broadcasts to his people over the BBC. On one occasion he is reported to have arrived by mistake at Bush House instead of Broadcasting House and approached the commissionaire who was not, of course, primed for his arrival. 'I am the King of Norway,' he said and the commissionaire busied himself on the telephone trying to find someone in authority to sort out the muddle. At one point he broke off and said,

'Er, 'scuse me, but where did you say you was King of?'

I was taking a wedding
for a couple. The groom had often said he was not
going to come to church, he didn't want all that
fuss. I opened:

*'Dearly beloved brethren, we are gathered here
in the sight of God and the fear of this
congregation . . .'*

REVD IAN C. HAWKINS, FAVERSHAM

A BBC foreign correspondent
reporting the 1973 October War in the Middle East
referred to the possibility of:

*'Lesbian forces moving down from the North
towards Israel.'*

8.25 FREE TO CHOOSE.
The case for free enterprise is
examined by Prof Milton Shulman
in the first of six programmes.
● The Daily Express

thousand peop

10.30 Thames I
which has bann(
in its schools, t

Quiet village

Oﾠne of our WRVS members
asked an old lady if there was anything she
wanted. She replied:

*'Yes, I'd like a long-sleeved Cardinal to keep
me warm.'*

MRS J. M. THOMASSEN, BEXHILL-ON-SEA

Dﾠavid Bellan,
presenting *Starsound* on Radio 2, said *à propos* a
record request:

*'I hope you're listening, Bernard, as your wife
tells me that 'Calamity Jane' will bring back
memories of your honeymoon.'*

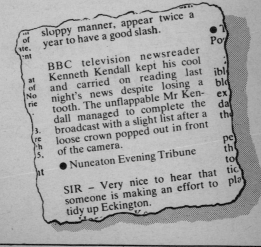

TYPEWRITER, portable Imperial in case, very little use, £12.
● Adscene

As a young girl
I was introduced by a friend at a party to a
formidable (to me – terrifying) uncle of his.
Proud at least to have remembered his name I said
ingratiatingly, 'How do you do, Mr Todd.' A
moment's awful silence ensued. Then my
friend said:

'Actually, it's Sweeney.'

KATHLEEN NEWELL, CHIGWELL

...sloppy manner, appear twice a
year to have a good slash.

BBC television newsreader
Kenneth Kendall kept his cool
and carried on reading last
night's news despite losing a
tooth. The unflappable Mr Kendall managed to complete the
broadcast with a slight list after a
loose crown popped out in front
of the camera.
● Nuneaton Evening Tribune

SIR – Very nice to hear that
someone is making an effort to
tidy up Eckington.

'*Dear Miss,*
Please excuse Sandra being late. She was
waiting for the bus at twenty to nine but came
back to use the toilet and missed it.'

'*Dear Miss Jones,*
Sorry Alan was away last week but with all the wet
weather he's had diarrhoea through a hole in
his shoe.'

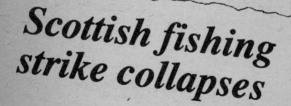

Scottish fishing strike collapses

SCOTTISH kippers admitted defeat as their three-week fishing
strike collapsed at the week-end.

● The Daily Telegraph

to

Abl

into th

BELL OUT OF USE

PLEASE USE KNOCKERS

To mark his sixtieth birthday, Prince Philip gave a radio interview in which he said:

'A few years ago everybody was saying we must have much more leisure, everybody is working too much. Now that everybody has got so much leisure — it may be involuntary, but they have got it — they are complaining they are unemployed. People do not seem to be able to make up their mind what they want, do they?'

WINDSOR CINEMA

ENDLESS LOVE

CANCELLED

Due to technical problems.

● South Wales Evening News

Arthur Calvert, beagle of the
York Gild of Freemen
● Yorkshire Post

When I was working
in a canteen one of the staff said:

*'You know why we are rushed off our feet?
Because they keep giving them those
luncheon vultures.'*

MRS J. GRIST, HAMPTON

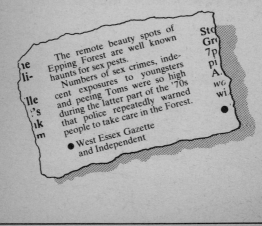

The remote beauty spots of
Epping Forest are well known
haunts for sex pests.
    Numbers of sex crimes, inde-
cent exposures to youngsters
and peeing Toms were so high
during the latter part of the '70s
that police repeatedly warned
people to take care in the Forest.

● West Essex Gazette
and Independent

FOR SALE recently acquired 2 second hand coffins, previous owner moving to warmer climate.

A local Mrs Malaprop spoke endlessly of her husband who suffered a lot with his 'slipped Dick'. She had been on holiday in a Carraway Van, the only complaint being that there was only one Emanuel Saucepan provided.

GERALD V. HALL, BATH

Wrong note!

Sir, – Thank you for including the article regarding my appointment as manager of the Twickenham branch of the National Westminster Bank on the retirement of Mr. Tom Bligh.

However, I would like to put the record straight in that my previous experience included "18 months with a foreign bank," not "18 years with a foreign band", as stated in your paper.

● Twickenham and Hampton Times

Three new members (including me)
of a well-known women's club had been asked by
the President to take coffee with her and be put at
our ease. We were indeed. She said:

*'Don't think the President is very special. Next
year I'll be nothing again, like you.'*

MARY PARKINS, NEW BARNET

I was in the company
of an elderly lady recently and there was some
argument as to the whereabouts of her airman son
at the end of the last war. Finally, to settle the
matter, she said:

*'Well, I know he was home on leave in May 1945
as we gave him a V.D. party.'*

KATHLEEN RICHARDSON, UXBRIDGE

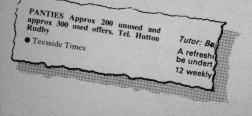

PANTIES Approx 200 unused and
approx 300 used offers. Tel. Hutton
Rudby
● Teesside Times

Tutor: Bo
A refresh
be undert
12 weekly

106

My dear old mother
and I were discussing a friend who had just left his
wife for a later model. She said:

*'I think it's disgusting. Where would he be
without her? Do you remember when he was
doing that PhD? She used to do all his typing –
and she used to sit up all night helping
him with his faeces.'*

BILL DUFFIELD, BANBURY

● The Post

2.40: 1
ible expl
blown
explosiv
daring s
the UK

7.00:
perform
this pe
to Blor
tion fo
play).

his home in
usband of
ral private.
evelopment
y.

Notes on the Program

Tone Poem, "Lemminkäinen's Return,"
Opus 22, No. 4 (from "Four Legends")
Born December 8th, 1865 in Ravastehus
Died September 20, 1857 in Jörvenpää
JEAN SIBELIUS

● Lincoln Center, New York.

:acefully at
d father of
uneral. No
l, to Marie
ane Street.

Y H. M. B.
de Guerre
her 848th
tters to 95,

pendent

111

Double Force

Velcro fastening

A show and a festival

The Royal Albert Hall stages, as always, the **Festival of Remembrance**: BBC1 (9.15 pm), and Radio 2 (8.30 pm) will be there. On Sunday the Cenotaph ceremony, including the two minutes' silence, can be seen on BBC1 and heard on Radio 4 (10.33 am).

8.2
An Evening in Vienna

Direct from the Spa Grand Hall, Scarborough

9.2 *Stereo*
Among Your Souvenirs

with Walter Midgley accompanied at the piano by Gladys Midgley, Lissa Gray, Harold Blackburn Balladiers, Clacton-on-Sea Co-Operative Band and the Reginald Leopold Orchestra
Introduced by **Alan Keith**
Producer ROBERT BOWMAN

9.5 *Stereo*
This Week's Composer

Palestrina
Mass: Assumpta est Maria
CHOIR OF ST JOHN'S COLLEGE, CAMBRIDGE
conducted by THE COMPOSER

● Radio Times

Don't kill yourself

108

S ir John Gielgud was lunching with the actress
Athene Seyler and fell to bemoaning his lot. 'I
spend all my time in the company of these old
bags of stage and screen – Monday, Fay Compton,
Tuesday, Sybil Thorndike, Wednesday, Athene
Seyler.' Then, realising what she might be thinking,
he quickly added:

'Of course, I don't mean you, Athene!'

Police put tail on 'dognap' gang

It was the classic kidnap. Mr
Sweeney was to take the ransom
money to a phone box near his home
and leave it inside a directory. It
would be picked up later. The ransom fitted easily inside the phone
book, for it was no great sum – just
£35. And Mr Sweeney was no mil-
lionaire grieving over a snatched
child.

The hostage was the Sweeney
family's pet dog Rufus.

The following morning Rufus, a
three-year-old pointer, was found
tied to a railing near his home.

Said a police spokesman: "We are
following certain leads.

● The Sunday Express

We were sorry to hear of the death of Miss Naomi Whelpton, a former Chichester Diocesan Moral Welfare Secretary (she was Mrs Shirley Emerson's predecessor). Miss Whelpton was trained at Josephine Butler House, Liverpool, and spent much of her time in this Diocese under Bishop Bell.

J ack Valenti,
President of the Motion Picture Association of America, was being interviewed on the radio about the pressures under which the United States President has to operate. He said:

'People nowadays want him to be knowledgeable about every tit and jottle of all sorts of subjects.'

Some years ago the children in my church organised an appeal to raise money to buy a guide dog for the blind. When all the money was in, arrangements were made to hand over the cheque to a representative of the association at a special service in church. As I made the presentation I heard myself saying:

'It gives me great pleasure, friends, to present this cheque to the association. The money the children have raised will buy a new blind dog for the guide...'

REVD J. DENNIS COPE, HARROGATE

THE TOP TWENTY MALAPROPISMS

1 'We've recently bought a beautiful three piece suite in stimulated leather...'

2 'Of course, we'll be quite comfortable, he's on a granulated pension.'

3 'There's nothing I like more on an evening like this than a long cool John Thomas.'

4 'I told him a hundred times it was no use, but it was like duck's water off his back.'

5 'His mother told him always to masturbate thirty-two times before swallowing.'

6 'He's in considerable pain because of his swollen tentacles.'

7 'My niece
is going to apply for a divorce because her
marriage has never been consumed.'

8 'He had to get
his biceps right down my throat.'

9 'And they brought gifts – Gold,
Frankenstein and Myrrh.'

10 'I simply cannot stand
the new vicar – he fornicates all over you.'

11 'Does your headmaster
believe in capital punishment in the
classroom?'

12 'I think he's bitten off a bit
of a white elephant there.'

13 'I've got this blouse
with Border Anglesey around the neck.'

14 'She was walking down the aisle carrying the most beautiful bunch of friesans.'

15 'Ee, I'll be glad to get back on terra cotta again.'

16 'And so we switched on the emotion heater and went to bed.'

17 'He's wonderful for his age, you know. He has all his facilities.'

18 'I often walk through the students' compost.'

19 'Well, the ball's in your frying pan now.'

20 'Don't fly off at a tangerine, lad.'

'Private Lives'

IT is as delightful to have a play again
at the **Duchess** (long occupied by
nudists) as it is to see a charming
revival of Noel Coward's "Private
Lives."

As I have boasted before, I peeded
over the side of my pram and actually
saw Coward and Gertrude Lawrence
create

● The Daily Telegraph

In Nottingham, travel agents

'**D**ear Miss,
*Our Johnnie came home with a big hole in his
trousers, will you please look into it.'*

'**D**ear Miss,
*I have not sent Johnny to school this morning
because he hasn't been. I have given him
something to make him go, and when he's been
he'll come.'*

In 1965, prior to a reception for Queen Elizabeth II outside Bonn, West Germany's President Heinrich Lübke, attempting an English translation of 'Gleich geht es los' (It will soon begin), told the Queen:

'Equal goes it loose.'

Three years earlier, Lübke had greeted the President of India at an airport by asking, instead of 'How are you?':

'Who are you?'

(To which his guest replied: 'I am the President of India.')

SOILED SPADES –
CHEAP

Anstey, Leicestershire

Priests

a time in prison could be a rewarding experience!

● The Church Times

Noel Coward, Beverley Nichols and Godfrey Winn were all invited to join Somerset Maugham at the Villa Mauresque to have lunch with the visiting American dramatist, Edna St Vincent Millay. As she swept on to the terrace overlooking the blue Mediterranean, she exclaimed:

'Oh Mr Maugham, but this is fairyland!'

Apathy

SIR – Very nice to hear that someone is making an effort to tidy up Eckington.

Here in Kempsey there appears to be a state of apathy. The roadsides are a mass of weeds, the footpaths are overgrown, the delightful pond has flotsam and jetsam abounding. The council, in the modern sloppy manner, appear twice a year to have a good slash.

What has happened to the old pondsman? Knock off an odd bureaucrat and bring him back.

W. H. Whitehead

● The Evening News, Worcester

£200 Greek urn stolen

A GREEK urn worth £200 was stolen from St Osyth Priory on Tuesday by a visitor looking round the old building.

The vase, which belongs to the De Chair family, who live at the priory, is described as pottery, about 18 inches high, with two purple handles edged in gold.

The main body of the vase is purple with gold insets of nude women, and it is about eight inches wide at the wildest point.

● East Essex Gazette

Worried Ousden residents are praying for a bridge over troubled waters. If work on

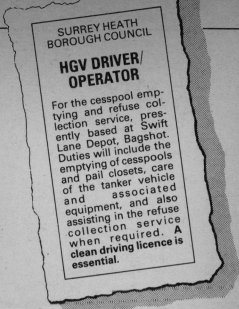

SURREY HEATH BOROUGH COUNCIL

HGV DRIVER/OPERATOR

For the cesspool emptying and refuse collection service, presently based at Swift Lane Depot, Bagshot. Duties will include the emptying of cesspools and pail closets, care of the tanker vehicle and associated equipment, and also assisting in the refuse collection service when required. **A clean driving licence is essential.**

Arrangements had been made for us to meet up with another couple to go out together. My wife who was dressed up to the nines blurted out, 'We thought you'd get dressed up.' There was an awkward silence and then one of them replied dismally:

'We thought we had.'

PETER NELSON, HULL

Two friends of mine
were with a group of people being shown round a
stately home in Shropshire. On entering a
particularly large room, the guide turned to his
audience and said:

*'This is where his lordship holds his balls
and dances.'*

IAN BURROW, TAUNTON

a bridge over troubled waters.

Joseph Conrad Walsh, 31, was found
guilty of indecent exposure and carrying an offensive weapon when he first
appeared at Redbridge Court on
March 5.

● Ilford Recorder

BUSINESS at a crematorium chapel came to a

"All you have to do is see a modest old lady undressing in a dormitory to realise that it is just not good enough and something must be done about it."

● Bridgnorth Journal

A MAN whose body was found in the sea at Penarth has been identified – almost
t...

Tutor: Bob Wright MBOU   **MIDLAND BIRDS**

A refresher course for old or new course members.
be undertaken in Rugby as well as other field visits. Detailed Tit study to   (EM)   Fee £6.00
12 weekly meetings from 30th September

● Rugby Review

7.30–9.30 p.m.

---

flowers, please, donations, if desired, to man
Curie Memorial Foundation, 199, Sloane Street.

A DOCTOR, whose bedside manner was said to have the makings of a slapstick comedy, was found guilty of serious professional conduct by the General Medical Council Disciplinary Committee yesterday.

● The Daily Telegraph

The justice ministry has demanded
a full 20

121

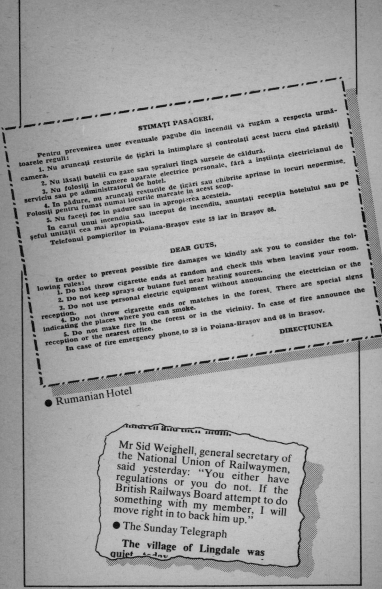

STIMAȚI PASAGERI,

Pentru prevenirea unor eventuale pagube din incendii vă rugăm a respecta urmă-
toarele reguli:
1. Nu aruncați resturile de țigări la întîmplare și controlați acest lucru cînd părăsiți
camera.
2. Nu lăsați butelii cu gaze sau spraiuri lîngă sursele de căldură.
3. Nu folosiți in camere aparate electrice personale, fără a înștiința electricianul de
serviciu sau pe administratorul de hotel.
4. In pădure, nu aruncați resturile de țigări sau chibrite aprinse in locuri nepermise.
Folosiți pentru fumat numai locurile marcate in acest scop.
5. Nu faceți foc in pădure sau in apropierea acesteia.
In cazul unui incendiu sau inceput de incendiu, anunțați recepția hotelului sau pe
șeful unității cea mai apropiată.
Telefonul pompierilor in Poiana-Brașov este 59 iar in Brașov 08.

DEAR GUTS,

In order to prevent possible fire damages we kindly ask you to consider the following rules:
1. Do not throw cigarette ends at random and check this when leaving your room.
2. Do not keep sprays or butane fuel near heating sources.
3. Do not use personal electric equipment without announcing the electrician or the
reception.
4. Do not throw cigarette ends or matches in the forest. There are special signs
indicating the places where you can smoke.
5. Do not make fire in the forest or in the vicinity. In case of fire announce the
reception or the nearest office.
In case of fire emergency, to 59 in Poiana-Brașov and 08 in Brașov.

DIRECȚIUNEA

● Rumanian Hotel

march and then mun.

Mr Sid Weighell, general secretary of
the National Union of Railwaymen,
said yesterday: "You either have
regulations or you do not. If the
British Railways Board attempt to do
something with my member, I will
move right in to back him up."

● The Sunday Telegraph

**The village of Lingdale was
quiet today.**

In the days of the Commonwealth Office,
the minister Arthur Bottomley paid a visit to
Zambia in December 1965. In his public
pronouncements he dismayed his hosts by
referring to the country as:

'Gambia.'

'**M**r Ronald Reagan has lost his head
over President Carter...er...Mr Ronald Reagan
has lost his <u>lead</u> over President Carter.'

BBC WORLD SERVICE NEWS, 20 AUGUST 1980

My wife, a school librarian,
was amused by the request of a rather small boy,
obviously sent by his teacher, who came into the
library and asked for a copy of:

'She Stoops to Conga.'

DAVID ALLSOPP, LONG EATON

'*In response to complaints
from the touring company of <u>Oh Calcutta</u>, the
nude revue, that they were suffering from the
cold, the theatre management has agreed to
install fan heaters.'*

BBC RADIO 4 NEWS, 12 DECEMBER 1981

Hubert Humphrey
commented on a failed attempt to assassinate
President Gerald R. Ford, thus:

*'There are too many guns in the hands of people
who don't know how to use them.'*

President Ford himself once commented:

*'Mr Nixon was the thirty-seventh President of
the United States. He had been preceded by
thirty-six others.'*

Golspie, Scotland

At my father's funeral, my step-mother had allowed one of father's friends to say "a few words" after the service was over. He started by saying that the last time he had been at that crematorium there had been some swallows flying about. He then went on to say how he had gone on bird-watching expeditions with my father, and so on. He ended (the cremation was taking place in early January) by saying:

'Now Mr G — and the swallows have departed to a warmer climate.'

REVD P. G., OXFORD

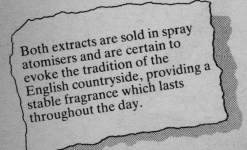

Both extracts are sold in spray atomisers and are certain to evoke the tradition of the English countryside, providing a stable fragrance which lasts throughout the day.

At the Royal Wedding in July, 1981, Lady Diana Spencer vowed: 'I, Diana Frances, take thee Philip Charles Arthur George to my wedded husband' – accidentally transposing the first two of his Royal collection of names. Not to be outdone, Prince Charles, instead of saying 'and all my worldly goods with thee I share' vowed 'with all *thy* goods with thee I share.'

While holidaying
in a small village in Scotland I was speaking to an
elderly inhabitant who had had a day out in
Edinburgh. At one point she said:

*'I wanted to cross the road, but I dinna ken how
to work the Presbyterian Crossing.'*

HELEN KERR GREEN, MARKET DRAYTON

'We are
examing alternative anomalies.'

WILLIAM WHITELAW, HOUSE OF COMMONS,
1 DECEMBER 1981

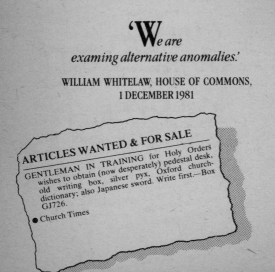

ARTICLES WANTED & FOR SALE

GENTLEMAN IN TRAINING for Holy Orders
wishes to obtain (now desperately) pedestal desk,
old writing box, silver pyx, Oxford church-
dictionary; also Japanese sword. Write first.—Box
GJ726.

● Church Times

In the December 1981
edition of *The Atlantic Monthly,* David Stockman,
Director of the Office of Management and Budget
in the Reagan Administration was quoted on the
following topics:

On Reaganomics:
*'The reason we did it wrong – not wrong, but
less than the optimum – was that we said, Hey,
we have to get a programme out fast . . . we
didn't think it all the way through. We didn't
add up all the numbers.'*

On the Administration's budget:
*'None of us really understands what's going on
with these numbers.'*

On defence spending:
*'The whole question is blatant inefficiency,
poor deployment of manpower, contracting
idiocy.'*

On his recommendations
for cuts in Social Security benefits:
'Basically I screwed up quite a bit.'

He offered his resignation.

'**W**e are going to play
a hiding and finding game. Now, are your balls
high up or low down? Close your eyes a minute
and dance around, and look for them. Are they
high up? Or are they low down? If you have
found your balls, toss them over your shoulder
and play with them.'

FROM A BBC 'MUSIC AND MOVEMENT' PROGRAMME FOR
CHILDREN WHICH, HAPPILY FOR POSTERITY, IS STILL ON
RECORD

Francesca Bellere is refusing to disclose the father's identity.

NEW YORK CURB ON GREEDY UNDERTAKERS
By Our New York Staff

Efforts are being made in New York to stop undertakers charging the earth for burials.

● The Daily Telegraph

Defender

In 1966, George Brown
who had formerly run the Department of
Economic Affairs was winding up for the Labour
Government in a debate on the economy in the
House of Commons. He declared earnestly:

*'For almost two years now we have tried to
manage the economy in a way that no economy
has ever been managed before.'*

Two mothers chatting
about a recently held Fancy Dress Party. One
asked: 'And did your little daughter enjoy
herself?'
The other replied:

*'Oh, yes, she looked very sweet. We dressed her
up in one of those Japanese commodes.'*

PAM FOX, WORPLESDON

One afternoon during the long,
hot summer of '76, a group of us were digesting a
large lunch. A large well-endowed lady with a
penchant for wearing loose thick wooly jumpers
complained that the heat was overbearing. I said:

*'That's hardly surprising. What do you expect
with your big sweaty floppers…?'*

JOHN CARTER, CARDIFF

I met a woman whose husband
was in hospital and asked how he was.
She replied:

*'Not good. They gave him a post mortem
yesterday.'*

JOAN HEWITT, MARYPORT

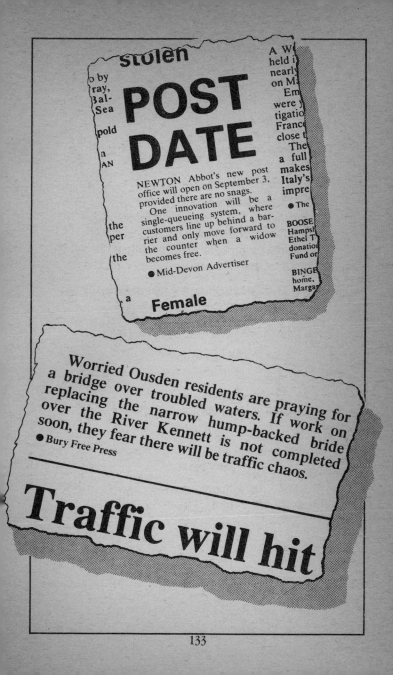

stolen

POST DATE

NEWTON Abbot's new post office will open on September 3, provided there are no snags.

One innovation will be a single-queueing system, where customers line up behind a barrier and only move forward to the counter when a widow becomes free.

● Mid-Devon Advertiser

Female

Worried Ousden residents are praying for a bridge over troubled waters. If work on replacing the narrow hump-backed bride over the River Kennett is not completed soon, they fear there will be traffic chaos.

● Bury Free Press

Traffic will hit

BLIZZARDS, snow drifts and icy roads have wrecked the county council highways budget and plunged Surrey into chaos.

Taken by surprise by one of the most severe winters of the century, finance chiefs are gritting their teeth.

● Surrey Advertiser

H er Majesty the Queen,
reading a speech during her Australian tour in
1977, referred to:

'The twenty-fifth reign of my year.'

(Shortly afterwards she started wearing
spectacles to read.)

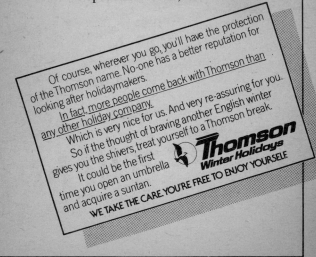

Of course, wherever you go, you'll have the protection of the Thomson name. No-one has a better reputation for looking after holidaymakers.

In fact, more people come back with Thomson than any other holiday company.

Which is very nice for us. And very re-assuring for you.

So if the thought of braving another English winter gives you the shivers, treat yourself to a Thomson break.

It could be the first time you open an umbrella and acquire a suntan.

WE TAKE THE CARE. YOU'RE FREE TO ENJOY YOURSELF.

Thomson Winter Holidays

Nice! Brucie is a grandad

ENTERTAINER Bruce Forsyth has become a grandfather.

His 22-year-old daughter, Julie, has given birth to a baby boy. She has named him Luke.

Bruce's latest addition to the generation game weighed in at 6lb 13 oz.

Luke's father, 29-year-old Dominic Grant, said: "It's terrific. I don't even know what lay it is."

● The Daily Mail

I cringe even as I write this down...
I was talking to a widow and asked her when her
husband died. She replied: 'Eleven years ago – on
12 August.' Without a moment's hesitation, – and
as the words sprang from my lips, I could taste
shoe-leather – I said:

'Oh – the Glorious Twelfth!'

PAUL JACOBSON, LEEDS

When I was in pantomine
at Peterborough, I had to run on the stage at a very
dramatic moment and announce to the King: 'Your
daughter has been taken away by gruesome
demons!' Instead, I rushed on stage and said:

'Your daughter has been taken away by
greesome nuemons!'

AUDREY LENO, EWELL

FAMILY
PLANNING.

PLEASE USE REAR
ENTRANCE

Barnstable Health Centre

In the 1930s
radio announcer Harry von Zell (who later
appeared in the Burns and Allen television shows)
was due to introduce a broadcast by President
Hoover. The words that actually came out of his
mouth were:

*'Ladies and gentlemen. The President of the
United States — Hoobert Heever!'*

A canticle is a sacred song used in church services and a New Testament canticle would be such a song deriving from the New Testament, e.g. 'My soul doth magnify the Lord'. One day at theological college some years ago, a lecturer marched in and announced he would address us on the subject of:

'New Cantament Testicles.'

REVD A. C. BETTS, LEEDS

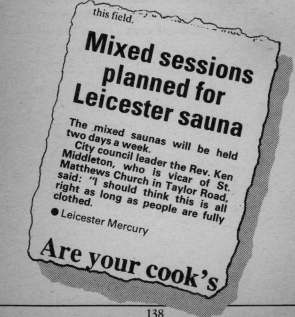

this field.

Mixed sessions planned for Leicester sauna

The mixed saunas will be held two days a week.

City council leader the Rev. Ken Middleton, who is vicar of St. Matthews Church in Taylor Road, said: "I should think this is all right as long as people are fully clothed.

● Leicester Mercury

Are your cook's

138

John Gielgud went to see the first performance of Richard Burton's *Hamlet*. According to the story, the performance was not of the highest but nevertheless Gielgud felt obliged to go back stage and congratulate Burton whilst concealing his true feelings about what he had seen. On entering Burton's dressing room, he discovered that the actor was in a state of undress. Gielgud meant to say, 'I'll come back when you're dressed.' What he is reported to have said, was:

'I'll come back when you're better...'

4.15 THE SKY AT NIGHT: Voyager 2 reaches Jupiter, with Patrick Moore.

● The Daily Mail

Leeds call girl raped. Man aids police

● Leeds Evening Post

Take the family to
**Birtsmorton Water
Foul Sanctuary near
Malvern**
● The Hereford Ad mag

At a promotional evening
for the Berlin Tourist Board, I was asked by a
German official, 'Have you ever been to Berlin?'
Without thinking, I heard myself answer:

*'No, but my father often flew over it
during the war.'*

LEN EDEN, BIRMINGHAM

CARTER ORDERED TO REST

By Our Washington Staff

President Carter was ordered to rest
by a doctor for what was described as
an aggravated problem with haemor-
rhoids.

A White House spokesman said
that Mr Carter had been in discom-
fort for several days and had been
told by his personal physician, Rear
Admiral William Lukash, to rest so
that he could seek relief from pain.

● The Daily Telegraph

en residents are praying

141

MANURE
75p per bag
DO IT YOURSELF
50p per bag

Sussex

An old lady
was telling her friend about a
'Good Companions' party:

*'And then they gave us some
Round-About-Eight-O'clock mints.*

WENDY HAMMOND, BOURNEMOUTH

The
open mouth invites the foot.

ANON

Dentopedalogy is the science
of opening your mouth and putting your foot in it.
I've been practising it for years.

PRINCE PHILIP

That is not what I meant at all.
That is not it, at all.

T. S. ELIOT, *THE LOVE SONG OF J. ALFRED PRUFROCK*

A *blooper*
is worse than a *goof*, more adult than a *boo-boo*,
not as serious as a *blunder*, equivalent to a *gaffe*.
Repeated commission of any results in a
description of having *Foot in Mouth Disease*.

WILLIAM SAFIRE, *SAFIRE'S POLITICAL DICTIONARY*